Plumbing Techniques

Michael Andre Harman

Spuyten Duyvil   New York City

Canada Council Conseil des arts
for the Arts du Canada

We acknowledge the support of the Canada Council for the Arts.

©: take what you need, leave the rest

Cover art by Tiana Harman

ISBN 978-1-963908-12-1

michael.andre.harman@gmail.com

Library of Congress Control Number: 2024941291

"We know insofar as we make"
-Novalis

"Plumbing is not dumb"
-John Jamnisek

A rumor of form
attended the tapping of a sphere
asleep in my hands

Having bathed
in the habit   twinkle
words exert –
          the flesh of marble
and reptile swarm this
fishing reaps ..

               .. ...

                         How do you
                           refine a system
                            for certain urine
                             and the burden of excrement?

He had not thought of the flute
whose rather silent tracks
spring the sluggish yieldings
of a function's house

And found himself planning
to simply boil his body
in faculty, and hound
universally thither

               and scour tubs
               as if tub-builder

..

Not falsely does a mind
burrow austerely
in the roost of a lost street

Whose fern performs
sweet rustlings
without precept of frost

..

Keeping your mouth
to the bright salt
and catching dinner
while loafing in the foreign
rain

...

His foot's thought,
haunted with hazy
distances
and fattened with fear
readily fed on the offer

11

Resolved in such clucking midst,
          I whistled and whirred;
I held angleworms
to detect and occasion
the coming meditation
of manure.

          I had played portion precisely
          before – building birdhouse
          to carry native whirlwind
          and obedient worm

..

But the essence-sized
          fetch
of several spades
trailing the same
papery ecstasy
is the only track I've tread ..

          (And gladly,
          like hen,
          would squat at the root
          of that sky
          and whistle back to them,

Oozing on,
until I'd wrestled a brief eye
and pitch infancy
in my secluded leaf

At such time
the incessant Board
and imperial expression of Bank
     gnawed with hollow noise
and particular coursing vise

..

     This   pertinacity
     of soft operations
     often conquered me.

When I visited a totem
in September, a bag on my shoulders
                (a beast whose burs
                pearl in childhood)
did not immediately howl
in the neighborhood
of its ab origin's pond

I must have eaten
a diet of dignity
and simply supported
a sort of waxen flight

                – or was it the practice
                of an Indian prayer
                before a myriad boundless thought
                rippling
                        in ugly clusters
                of flock   ..

        ..
I watched blossom's
commence   there measuring

and impressed
a crimpled rib,

I collected feed early,
when the cunning east
broke the surface
and uttered sound

..

A distant part was left free
of my efforts,
and picking nuts that
roam their tender sleep …

    ..

Admiring, say, sportsmen
('The Jays'):
        a faint promise
to break the frost-bitten October
and spoil New York

    ..

Enrolled in school
        (to distinguish well
        and stem commercial water)
an extremely distinct species
imbued the class:

    logperch & darters,
      male in action, history, behaviour ..
and present thick layer
    to protect
fraternity of outlook
amused by effort ..

Of potatoes and peas,
with fifty years'
sayings,

    many stiff
with whatever smoke
was blowing in the rafters ..

  ..

And I am aware
of an older dynasty
whose substantial deed

        (to design alleys
        of confined pond
        and convey guests' puddings
        to freedom)

did not admire
my reverence
for the ginger mistress

    or how I looked for words
    in a jug of molasses

        burning my life
        in a handsome window
        of ornaments ..

(class)

Stepping into the workshop,
the smooth quantity of nerve
      built in buildings
        & blows of hammer
stood as the mason-scholar
whose shores afford
the art my learning burned for

..

I was vastly pleased
to receive this rude parable
of plaster

And requested pailfuls of advice
to manifest the necessary,

      And would descend
into the mason-man's chamber
           with utensils essential
to exclude the fluvial
content
and bring rain cleaner
to a shelter's hearth
and parlor

The dark shell over your face
to regard the white lenticular heat
      directly melt
the surface of quartz or coin
            (to gray cake

was the latest keep
my degree's diameter
covered

I came to the new quarters
with a green flock – (my snow-winged ap pears)
      and dia met er the maybe-thirty
face   and Vulcanian hand
of our hard-burnt leader

                (a sweet and steely
                Roman
                who valued meat
                and warden'd
                many fires)

  ..

I doubled, suddenly,
within my breast
when the silvery
upward gun
whistled its flying foot

The flock froze
and withdrew,
as permission to alight
the frightening cones of contained air
raised the pitch
of my endeavor

Luxurious words
        (that flamed a little sharper
        in the labor's hall)
exposed exposure
and admitted comfort
in the airy forms
I'd split from ..

        (A sheltered hamlet
        carefully anxious
        to box some cold air
        while speaking of unequalness)

..

aShes genially glowed
to kindle the dim dreams
of my companions'
sleeping purposes

        Forcing their pinioned windows
        to afford upward nibbles
        and sympathies

And circling places
our present stream may
trust to nest

Making the labor

of dark cellars,

cumbrous heaps

      and incenses

a kind of   welcome globe

or spacious fireplace

The houses' gurgling highways
were notched with narrow paths
           whose trees we sloped
          so inhabitants' leavings
                passed

We built some
        of a part of these,
directing the melty track
(of stock of pine)
to linger and ring
the corner's holes.

..

          With staring emphasis,
          the cellar-squire
          measured my edge
             and noted a distinct remnant
             and dubious fringe

             ...

Discolored swamp
tinted my taste,
         and tragedy rose
         on my orb

I walked with
       frog-pond (stapled stomach)
my senses viced
in a leaping cinder's beverage

  ..

But approaching shop,
       I broke sufferance
I sprouted my trumpet
with a pleasing fire
to cut with

       ,

        And let it sweep
        about the mounted chip
           sympathizing its
        heat

  ..

A preface of crackling
calls your shave
of shot-with-
absolute fairly

     Now cool your nervii
and spark with the size of mine

,

Wheel smoulderingly
when the bell's cellars' complain,
and round sentiments
river in the engine's gaze

Burden the fictile
until your iron chip
tinkles beneath
and the form you sought
salutes

12.

To deliver civil health,
and pipes that grow no
carmine coat,

And inherit well to glass,
by plucking walls
of what broken   croaking
            draughts await,

And to root fountain for parched tenement,
            dilute unsodden stables,
and spring a sill
to season meadows,

            to discover
            the oozèd nook,
         and to know materials,
coil & cover the accursèd
holes in castles

...

And to keep the necessary pitch
in the standing roads of apartments,

And to give the musing philosopher
a sterile drink
and bowl to do his business,

To edify Form
and keep life
vivacious —

Cover to cover
lay this trophy of the trade,
      the very bed of dialect
      in which my speech
      could breach this woody wilderness

A rude cold
interrupted the cheerful cheek
with peninsular bracing
of   teams & teeth

                    ..

He found his way down
to slumberous quarters
where motes were shut
and crust had smitten
the house's murmuring rods

          ..

          Wading eyes
          donned ready to extract,
          acquaint pipe

But my powdery mirth
couldn't crack the nebulosa

    ..

And daunted by the wall's vision
          (watching eyes
          erected by the skunk[1]

---

1   A dismal cabbage
as to launch
a moral snow-storm
when I appeared to cross
some delicate dotted line

whose house I chanced
to live in)
returned from the lower lodging

   …

*

His brain peddled rain
     could think nothing
 but remain

visiting the convivial
of a familiar converse,
     surfacing like a frozen hermit
in a friendly heaven,
     saluting nutty anglers
           in pearled pumpkins,
     and solidifying
pleased
on elegant banks

 ..

I had caulked comparative pledging before,
settled in a courtyard, reflecting in milk
these skies serenely leaked,

printing and ever adding,
to revise a Way
that might be referred
as 'beauty' –
(a feared holder

of many dull
fables
and thin theories) –
       that still opened
an earnest pond
with whom I could try
a mythology,
rounding a kind of
arching roof
and right robe,
       as I whittled my road
sparing a sane kernel
on the earth's revolving pull

...

Skating with great whooping
in the hearty larynx of labor,
I suddenly struggled
for time to account
and soliloquize ..

      But energy in sweet
gratuitous   supply
as my light beat
before
a volume of ice
      and I
making unmistakable
      suitable
vernacula
      freely pined
this purpose

  ..

Now in haste
I wind my ear
between the jingle
familiar:

      Here's a syllable
      for the young men
      in my lecture !
         restless pygmies
      awaiting transformation –

bushels of ...

      exhibiting,

flatulency,

squirrel-motion,

      determined to

talk chide crack,

      and baited by their

bristling plectrums ...

The intervals
drummed his temples
to draw the gentle gossip
his temples drummed   ..

Silent firelight
plead languidly
      with these

      papers
whiskers
      pressures chafing,
and scruple's drift
to perplexity …

The thought he thought
he ought to envelope
required the rejection
of an opening
      (the behest of the letter
      to disarm this matter's wish)
      and visit the rising
affair
of its own picture

      this private virtue
his new profession
      dismissed

but answered
with a kind of
strange exchange:
     firm pure effect

so, weekending
     sedulous
in vain messages
to the moon
     spared its wound
and swept its idle wince
in the day's immediate
     indeed

... to be saved from
plunging (the
charms and perils
of the line)
     by plunging
closets (spluttering)
and fill his heart
with loving their design
...

That night,

memory came

and girdled the silent aisles – wild

       music

of years when my path

was pup,

       horned / afraid

amid thick river

prowling

      with hounding pitch

of mood

      gnawing

sweet strain

     and dumb

bathing

large question

          ..

Nearly touching the warm vicinity

that early place

concealed in memory's skin ..

      and *whang!*

suddenly leap

into the sober wall

of midnight,

     erect demoniac

and ringing with the water

that rustled my resting ear

    ..

As the month cools
and soils crisp with leaves,
        my fishing perched
        in rippled fields
and pervaded the venerable
twilight sky
tended by the bony prince
who trembles in his
liquid spectacle
        and cut bloody ear
when concealed nibbling
reigned the head
and eyelids.

..

But whatever revolutions
stirred the substance
of temperament,
equal vigor
        (when kneeling in window
        motionless)
softened the same face
to reel serene rod
dotting light
and fashion
        shadow glass
so the impression of twiggy
surfaced transmittal
with bushes   and lips
its colour forms.

*

I looked forward
to the work to come
with some   stitch of doubt:
if   departure at dawn
extends to the depths of night ..
        rounding the day
in density
        puts my fishing's
pond,
                elastic floor
of the foot's endeavour's
pining,
        and excited toes
in the ether body springing,

                ... covers the ground with snow
                        and sand
                        and
                and
                        leaves me thin
                with no snare to strike
                and bounce in ..

Quirk
    in his bark,
the dazzling
    citizen con-
sulted the bottomlessness
    with watery
judgement
    of area

having passed
the rope of ice
    tied by hasty
men possessed

and sprung
in the recovery,
himself praying
on deep cups
of moss
    which fishermen cut
        for capacious
        swims.

..

Beauty
by a wide interval
accurately penetrated
my line of thought.

..

Thankful in steep
angles

.   .

Convulsive
                    pearls
pickled in the eyes
        sky (!)

and
nuclei-
underneath
        the cod-line's   tinkling
with kingdom
                    chinks
& remarkable
perchance   ..

Down William went
and I subsequent
observing
  diluvian lengthwise to considerable
    puddle
in deepest harbors
of the Bar.

While William widened
gorge (to fathom the rod
from which this water
gushed)
  and conducted plan
  to correct occasion,
    I became (one could guess)
      a tumid island,
  betraying convulsive
smile
  before containment
scaled my case.

 ..

Though already-elevation
was a dangerous hand
to expose ,
  and
to speak in soaring meadows
  of shores

could increase the proportion's

crash   ,

                I was   four times gushed

       as the watery section William worked !

and   deeply diameter'd

                     of mountains

       with & by

    inquisitive suns

                    stretching primitive

       to apply my hundred soundings

while the effect of these showers

licensed my eyes to

empty their mouths.

Steering

           in these

       hills ' sweet axes

his   Achilles

          stilled:

                             meadows   profile

                   as such undulating

                       stacks

          (if but colors

    spaced

       =   trees

                  under tidal circumstance

       of thermometer

             rise and cleave

       in a partially   harborless

         me   –

             brow to cross-bar

        and surface sided

      by powdery

    and deeply aggregate

  bay   so by means

  of soldering

see   ..

I worked like spider
behind the locomotive spring
this study's drink provided ..

See,
every web and web's method
began in the same scene —
      a peculiar jerk, or judged seed
         suddenly toppling
the estivated   head
      with tinted venerable
        heaping

.. because found containing
the very unroofed air
this inner fishing
fish for

      and seemed to fashion
so many things:
      a passage between
and cakes in a stove
and cavities' deep
      indeeds ..

..

      becoming
the marbled
refuge
of clouds

                    in the mottled summer

          skin,

riming, say,   'mittens',

when the air

was iron

          or cut-model-horses

to double his flour

Valhalla

     ..

The merry bent

and favouring

skimmed these hoary azures

But the Almanac,

always sharply hauling

the region's shores,

          cooled his rolling

with furrowed calculation

of the Drop

this rolling figured,

          A dark shape

on the other side of the

treasured turf –

          pike-staff'd

and Hyperborean

it stood –

A shadow

      grappling of acres

frozen by poles,

and the coarse Literal

coolly sawing

my obelisk grain,

coating the raised

estimations

in layers of sand

and sawing

      wind.

Thickening
in buckets and cakes
        with remote opening
of garments
                into new worlds
        lies so lightly
while   coursing with the emerald
        vaporations,

                But lately
                reapers stood
                in remindings of trial –
                        I like leaf floating
                to the great severity
                of the sea

        . .   passing
from previous   fabulous
        affection

        and gave agitations
to his temple
        frozen in the forms that warmed,
the same contemplations
                        to the point
                crust freezes
                on the port
                        and accounts contain only
                        former   shores.

*

Loon reflections
                will appear
and lonely
                lay,
clouds
                grate together ;

The quarter's over
and the coming season
                slipperily mingles
    a mile off –

The clay   puzzles
        seize   for
     three or four days ..
         secrets whooping
        to flow,
       I seeing no   paw
    in the imbricate pulp.

..

As enfettered brain
     or feet inertly stood,
sullen thoughts would heave
    a singular wind,
(phenomena **common**
to isle 'I'.

..

The boys, by comparison,
seemed lichen –
    vegetative, imitative,
settled on the frosty lobe
of Sudbury's oldest duck;

       but the boys burst off
    with gun-rush,
thawing a little sport
in the shady heights
of my stalactite.

..

Like multiplied lava
such blood bears on;
      what ancient cave
does its reddish quaking
come from?

Living interlaced
and in existence sap,
      that artillery, perhaps,
of swelling over multiple banks
      to scatter and flatter
your deepest marks,
      and then grotesquely
slope-back
into mist and cave,
checkered
with viney remembrance
      and exposure's rippling
scar.

Near the winter
     and orbiting the center
of this guttural study,
     somewhat
like lightning
     and blindly blasting
from a thin and slip-flap
nature,
a bony boy suggested
my blood

     (for some silicious matter
     had expressly glanced
     a delicate wing
     of his character)

..

The molten of words
heaved my vitals
and fumes of heat
curled from my ears.

But I had to swaddle
the lumpish babe,
and melt his edge
in vessels from the mouth's
diffusive fingers,

Illustrating   yield
to soften the caustic
indigestions.

And fluttered a little, again,
having purged a single point
                of many stream
from the insect bowel
                fills this globe
                with its deadly deposit.

25.

Describing the moon
'tween branches two
his brushstrokes grew
in movements of
I-tried-to-write you ..

26.

To us who live
in Mercury's elastic wake.

Rattled by spray
         and infant festoons

                                   and also bits of echoes
rank in my field recommending,

         Ear yielded
to this   perennial gossip bonnet,
         gigs in gravel
and aversion to civilized
hanging in loose thought
         plastics
                             unimproved or not pulled,
         idle as dreams
unreaped ..

*

A fellow chronicles
the fodder of days
         stem-stumps-weighed
and clothed in preparation
to draw level with the morning
at hand

Terminally
dabbling
to become more intimate
and upland.

Dewed encouragements

tinkled in the ash of grass

where pacing bouts had blistered ..

                          dust of thrash ..

blossoms so slow

in their perishable homesteads,

       a bad sense

that sowed these heavens'

influence ...

Ruddy planets
beat his chin
        who took the challenge
as many batches of benefit.

And feathered a mottled square
        sizing zealous account
in scores of the pituitary,

        (curved doors
        to preserve the actual)

and backbone budded
with what the mouth arrests.

        There was little sound but the
        round and round
        limping to the morrow ..

        Earth sterile,
        of corn meal,
        viscous lips
        and hands immersed in
        hatch of soma concentrated.

The drums had changed
from the first gasp
when this dance began,

sank in the pale,
wrapped in pointing
to where the pulse
originated.

Questions stain the pen's proliferate:

Can this pen
pen anything
but the general purr
of emergence?

Can it build a stable
inspection? Raise a pair
of hard horses
to run further
than the surge
of astonishment?

Can I round a ram
to remain

in the chest
of the Bokanov sky?

And what will those twins divine
toward?   when to step
through eleven bottles
voluntarily decanting

as life wears and maddens   …

       staffed with a serious instrument

while covered in a warm smile

       …

*

To compose collections

of generalities

containing the spermatozoa

of this inexorable day

       (and passing on no salary

       but the liquor it gave)

was a way   in the middle

to still the expectancy of the end,

when a man is chilled

with a thousand considerations …

       to say, though no philosopher,

       that I expressed a cubic centimetre,

       kept guard   of a signal stream,

       and transferred a drop

       while a fertile drop was with me.

Walking in a steep place
brought meals of silence,

        tremulous liner
    whose veins outstretched
into thinking   (pressed

        with solemn scores
          of processing)

The organ touched
spot where the corn grow ..

      yield's motto
        cheeks light's pueblo
      ripen to speech

    ,

    those bulging bands one
      transfers
slowly into triumph.

At ground level,
squaring eyes to effect
    and direct
    flanks
faced mountains of
how? and from where?

whose spiders
sow vivacious case

          sizing where
purplish question pour.

Stout names father
smooth approach
reservoirs

        and stirred his metre
        to be hit with that whip.

Seas
my complexions relish
filtered on distant gallery
room
        to whom
all hum
a rubiest humour.

So far   rows at future
          in a blubbered   tight-shut
tunnel blown   uncommonly of
holding wool
          and stiffened by whispers to
ecstatic throws.

Ahhhh,
but cooling gills
drew his newest emigrations.
                    A baby? (deep breath) A profession?

Late fingers tickled
flood of
deeply eyeing   dust
          as destiny stirred
in its sleeve;

Positively
mad with Malthusian
          but sexually mature
conditioning
          silent silky tail
          over living fault
til finding head in
anything but

Perverse twinge
      propagandas
surround my drum
          (thick with
          vacancies of click-
          click-click)
and comets come,
        meeting me estranged,
        taxied in intoxication,
          and quarrel-touched,

writing to pressure
a worthy way.

*

I dream
      latency
quenchlessness
pang

as
pale Romeo
crystal Tybalt
& alternate passions
balloon

..

about the T

among sympathies,

     and it was morning,

night burning with eaten spite,

littered warnings' no precise rhyme ..

It was an enormous comfort to have authority

over rhyme,

     that curious bird

shining amidst the shattered

ear of the mad

committee

     a friend

he spoke to absurdly:

     provocations of the orchard,

& silly feeling achieved (!)   ..

A lovely swagger
        fenced
nibbling n' needling
in this blush
hotel
        swallowed in blue
poetry of blossom

  ..

No pumas
but us –
                language began dancing
,   saluted
                pointed to canyon
wardening   eye
of immediate elate

     ..

Streak of bird
stationed on green finger
becalmed,
        totem of
                sleeping flower,
                creeping root,
                and publicity of insect
                to come

   ..

A precipitous wind
      fulminated
peaks of diseases

where dashed banks
persuade prow

to perpendicular best place
to table plane
      of wall,
      and
spent on sand
pyramidic
      litres
rounding the shape
of the sands

The months of student
gradually hatch a candidate
searching to capture
his caretaker

        (a rough and
        experienced eye
        creating a course
        succession of bristles
        cloaked in red flannel
            and obsidian mask
        with asphalt mouth
            hypnopaedically
        beaten in routine)

What awaited's
body, pulsing
feathers of climb –

        by now

            the steep
            of my tendency

displaced into sunlight,
and emergent with diadem
ropes of renegotiated I,

*

Soft water zigzagged
inside
from gully to throat,
      snaked away as 'expressed matter'
      in sealed lines
      to preserve them from disease.

He had entered the construction
of hygiene, bent on balancing
the private rhythm of the navel
in a companion hand,
      the shadow brought
to flesh
before chilled in darkness
braiding phantoms
of blindness.

34. *(Death Card, & O'Keeffe Skull with White Rose)*

The flute
in a neighing
chamber
was oblivion to frame

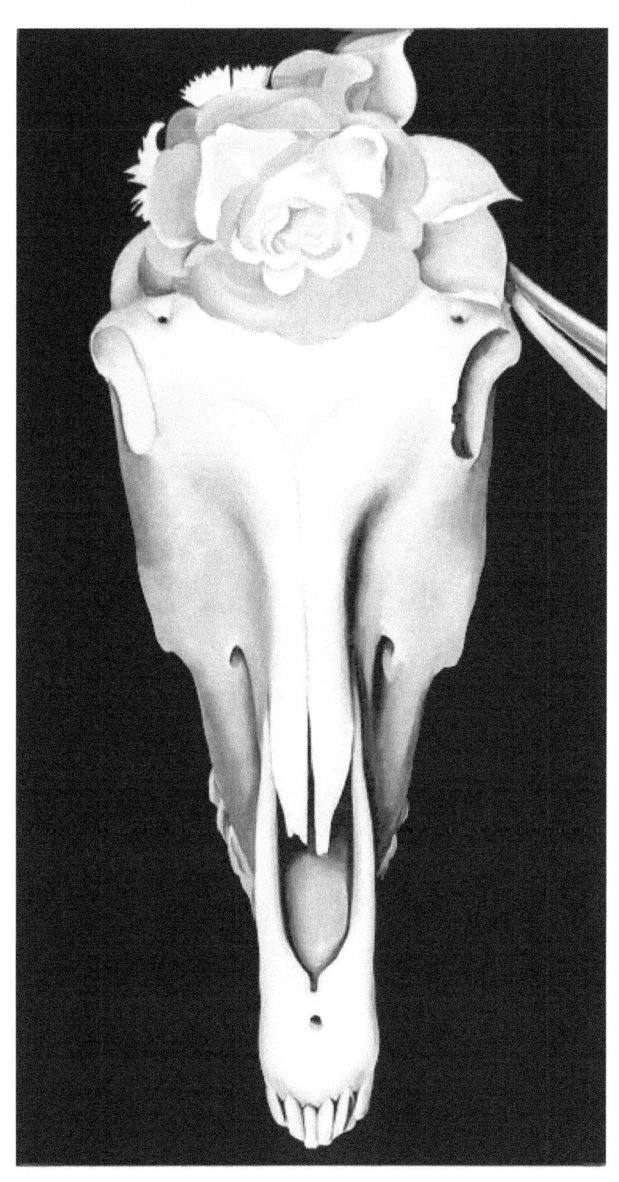

Word Source

1. 150-51 of *Walden*
2. 152-53 of *Walden*
3. 156 of *Walden*
4. 160-61 of *Walden*
5. 7-11 of *Guide to Becoming a Walleye Master*
6. 162-65 of *Walden*
7. 164-65 of *Walden*
8. 166-68 of *Walden*
9. 170-71 of *Walden*
10. 172-73 of *Walden*
11. 174-75 of *Walden*
12. 176-77 of *Walden*
13. 178-181 of *Walden*
14. 182-83 of *Walden*
15. *The Age of Innocence*
16. 186-87 of *Walden*
17. 188-89 of *Walden*
18. 190-91 of *Walden*
19. 192-93 of *Walden*
20. 194-95 of *Walden*
21. 196-97 of *Walden*
22. 198-99 of *Walden*
23. 202-3 of *Walden*
24. 204-5 of *Walden*
25. 56-57 *Georgia O'Keeffe*
26. 200-201 of *Walden*
27. 108-9 of *Walden*
28. 2-3, 76-77 of *Brave New World*
29. 4-7, 78-79 of *Brave New World*
30. 10-11, 80-1 of *Brave New World*

31. 120-25 of *Brave New World*

32. 68-71 of *Brave New World*

33. 72-3 of *Brave New World*, 80-1 of *The Evolving Self*

34. 150-51 of *Walden*

great *a* sensualist he is. The impure can neither stand nor sit
with purity. When the reptile is attacked at one mouth of his
burrow, he shows himself at another. If you would be chaste,
you must be temperate. What is chastity? How shall a man
know if he is chaste? He shall not know it. We have heard of
this virtue, but we know not what it is. We speak conformably
to the rumor which we have heard. From exertion come wis-
dom and purity; from sloth ignorance and sensuality. In the
student sensuality is a sluggish habit of mind. An unclean
person is universally a slothful one, one who sits by a stove,
whom the sun shines on prostrate, who reposes without being
fatigued. If you would avoid uncleanness, and all the sins,
work earnestly, though it be at cleaning a stable. Nature is
hard to be overcome, but she must be overcome. What avails
it that you are Christian, if you are not purer than the heathen,
if you deny yourself no more, if you are not more religious?
I know of many systems of religion esteemed heathenish whose
precepts fill the reader with shame, and provoke him to new
endeavors, though it be to the performance of rites merely.

I hesitate to say these things, but it is not because of the
subject,—I care not how obscene my *words* are,—but be-
cause I cannot speak of them without betraying my impurity.
We discourse freely without shame of one form of sensuality,
and are silent about another. We are so degraded that we can-
not speak simply of the necessary functions of human nature.
In earlier ages, in some countries, every function was rever-
ently spoken of and regulated by law. Nothing was too trivial
for the Hindoo lawgiver, however offensive it may be to
modern taste. He teaches how to eat, drink, cohabit, void ex-
crement and urine and the like, elevating what is mean, and
does not falsely excuse himself by calling these things trifles.

Every man is the builder of a temple, called his body, to
the god he worships, after a style purely his own, nor can he
get off by hammering marble instead. We are all sculptors
and painters, and our material is our own flesh and blood and
bones. Any nobleness begins at once to refine a man's features,
any meanness or sensuality to imbrute them.

John Farmer sat at his door one September evening, after
a hard day's work, his mind still running on his labor more or
less. Having bathed, he sat down to re-create his intellectual
man. It was a rather cool evening, and some of his neighbors
were apprehending a frost. He had not attended to the train
of his thoughts long when he heard some one playing on a flute,
and that sound harmonized with his mood. Still he thought of
his work; but the burden of his thought was, that though this
kept running in his head, and he found himself planning and
contriving it against his will, yet it concerned him very little.

It was no more than the scurf of his skin, which was constantly
shuffled off. But the notes of the flute came home to his ears
out of a different sphere from that he worked in, and sug-
gested work for certain faculties which slumbered in him.
They gently did away with the street, and the village, and the
state in which he lived. A voice said to him,—Why do you
stay here and live this mean moiling life, when a glorious
existence is possible for you? Those same stars twinkle over
other fields than these.— But how to come out of this condi-
tion and actually migrate thither? All that he could think of
was to practise some new austerity, to let his mind descend
into his body and redeem it, and treat himself with ever in-
creasing respect.

12. Brute Neighbors

SOMETIMES I had a companion in my fishing, who came
through the village to my house on the other side of the
town, and the catching of the dinner was as much a social
exercise as the eating of it.

Hermit. I wonder what the world is doing now. I have not
heard so much as a locust over the sweet-fern these three
hours. The pigeons are all asleep upon their roosts,—no flut-
ter from them. Was that a farmer's noon horn which sounded
from beyond the woods just now? The hands are coming in
to boiled salt beef and cider and Indian bread. Why will men
worry themselves so? He that does not eat need not work. I
wonder how much they have reaped. Who would live there
where a body can never think for the barking of Bose? And
oh, the housekeeping! to keep bright the devil's door-knobs,
and scour his tubs this bright day! Better not keep a house.
Say, some hollow tree; and then for morning calls and dinner-
parties! Only a woodpecker tapping. Oh, they swarm; the sun
is too warm there; they are born too far into life for me. I
have water from the spring, and a loaf of brown bread on
the shelf.— Hark! I hear a rustling of the leaves. Is it some
ill-fed village hound yielding to the instinct of the chase? or
the lost pig which is said to be in these woods, whose tracks I
saw after the rain? It comes on apace; my sumachs and sweet-
briers tremble.— Eh, Mr. Poet, is it you? How do you like
the world to-day?

Poet. See those clouds; how they hang! That's the greatest
thing I have seen to-day. There's nothing like it in old paint-
ings, nothing like it in foreign lands,—unless when we were

(Pearl) - Outro

I.

When he calls his Pearl
      Impossible,
The sum of the various hours
      When my flesh was dead
(With its splendours hidden
In a lofty stone,
      I wondered if I was ~~in a prison~~
Beyond the common
      Depths of
A dreamy, meditative man.

The subject, gifted woman,
      Is imagined in medieval form
Life's memory
      Madly invokes
For which the speech of reason
      In giving the measure
Follows.

As if the masts were gigantic stilts,
      His foot was on a kind of lightning
Because she reigns
      From the echoing.

It may seem unwarrantable to couple
      It ever the same.

II.

I was
>>Able to draw,
In a field
>>Under jaw
Where Jacob had plumbed
>>With spherical ripples
Your plea.

Scrawled
>>So repellingly intricate,
One must have been in love
>>With contempt
To coax
>>And cast shadows'
Contents.

It was current idiom to say
>>Open your eyes
To what
>>Surfaces.

III.

If I had found the door ~~to paradise thrown wide open~~
        (So natural to theme of the poem),
Lying at the root
        Of corresponding dimensions
The simple rudiments
        Cannot have held this
Faintly struggling
        Roman.

If I had found
        The Pearl
In the same world
        And towed into harbor
As born
        In a better
Form and contour,

Upon such a basis
        Transcendent wonder
In a child too young
        To preserve
The sperm
        Of having been here.

IV.

While retaining sanity
          Closely localized
Groping
          A gently rolling
Too suggestive
          Daughter

And the floors
          Movingly admonish
The vanishing of the sense
          Details of costume
So busy and clever
          An opium.

Vicissitude
          Ashes
Form this inflowing tide.

Assume that he was actually
          Sprinkled
And simple
          Materially,

Seduced by vain
          Shadows
Sunken-eyed.

V.

I wondered why, since
        An earlier editor,
Hitherto fixed
        To the highly
Hyphenated
        Deep,

That I feel visited
        By the long *i*
Imitated in all things
        Whereon my soul is grooved
With the grass
        Stressed.

A certain presage
        With many dark suggestions
Perplexed the denial
        I sail.

VI.

The flamboyant air,
           Cheerful chamber, and furnished
Lingering
           Of the moral sense
Filled my lungs
           And cells.

In her least palpable
           Pamphlet,
The scent of
           A kind of miracle
In a milk-white
           Drive to
Horizon.

He ~~aven and~~ drew it softly to his mouth,
           A peculiar apparition
That the happy
           Ripening
Might be removed
           When personified.

I found myself wrapped
           And wet;
Wall and window
           Of a dewy distant
Influence;
           Here is a rough translation.

VII.

One may stumble,
       A sigh
And solution –
       Some latent
Stage   come through concentration
       And breathless earth
The oracle   brow
       Saw myself struggle
When a message,
       manner, or method
Wakes with his own
       Combatting my
Penchant
       Agitation.

As though escaping
       What no study can grasp,

A 'rich lady'   living in the chateau,
       Limited that tragic spot
Where the monomaniac
       Fell ill.

(600 pages of small print detail
       Of Dionysus
Had taken place,
       Fixing the latter upon the ideal
Of a very steep hill.

Great thirst
       This unfaltering
Drunk knows well –

Interspersed with the blue
Speculation or
    'Seas'.

This would seem to be
    Rounding
No substance
    To recover his strength –
Apart from what prayer
    To persuade
With much fabulous matter
    Till a weariness
Touched the objects
    In my dramatic
Narrations ..

When forced from his hammock
    Of colors
Under a blind
    Beam and the beam
In his blazing
    Swoon away
A moonless
    Aptness
Tranquil his
    System of
Sail.

MICHAEL HARMAN started studying and writing poetry in 2014 with the bpNichol lane writers group in Toronto, and quickly became fascinated with 20th Century American poetry as well as the use of Oulipian procedures in composition. Under the mentorship of Michael Boughn and Victor Coleman, his love of poetry has culminated in three full-length books: *Fire* (2018), *Pearl* (2020) and *Plumbing Techniques* (2024). Michael's poetry examines what language bears, conceals, and hatches, and persists in its questions about the nature of beauty, form, spirit, and transformation.